CHICAGO
WHITE SOX

by George Castle

Published by ABDO Publishing Company, 8000 West 78th Street, Edina, Minnesota 55439. Copyright © 2011 by Abdo Consulting Group, Inc. International copyrights reserved in all countries. No part of this book may be reproduced in any form without written permission from the publisher. SportsZone™ is a trademark and logo of ABDO Publishing Company.

Printed in the United States of America,
North Mankato, Minnesota
112010
012011

Editor: Matt Tustison
Copy Editor: Nicholas Cafarelli
Interior Design and Production: Carol Castro
Cover Design: Christa Schneider

Photo Credits: Mark Duncan/AP Images, cover; Beth A. Keiser/AP Images, title; Amy Sancetta/AP Images, 4, 10, 43 (bottom); David J. Phillip/AP Images, 7; Kevork Djansezian/AP Images, 9; AP Images, 12, 15, 16, 18, 20, 23, 25, 29, 30, 33, 42 (top and middle); File/AP Images, 26, 42 (bottom); Charles Knoblock/ AP Images, 34; Photo by Ronald C. Modra/Sports Imagery/ Getty Images, 37; Charles Krupa/AP Images, 38, 43 (top); Charles Rex Arbogast/AP Images, 41, 43 (middle); Henny Ray Abrams/AP Images, 44; Nam Y. Huh/AP Images, 47

Library of Congress Cataloging-in-Publication Data
Castle, George.
  Chicago White Sox / by George Castle.
     p. cm. — (Inside MLB)
  Includes index.
  ISBN 978-1-61714-039-6
  1. Chicago White Sox (Baseball team)—History—Juvenile literature. I. Title.
GV875.C58C375 2011
796.357'640977311—dc22
                            2010036559

TABLE OF CONTENTS

CHAPTER 1

DON'T STOP BELIEVIN'

Every team should experience a dream season once in their fans' lifetimes. For the Chicago White Sox and their long-suffering fans, that year was 2005.

The White Sox had not won a World Series since 1917. They were a seemingly unlucky franchise. Perhaps their best team, the 1919 squad, gave baseball a black eye with the infamous "Black Sox" betting scandal. The Sox's 1959 Fall Classic appearance ended in a six-game loss to the Los Angeles Dodgers. It was their only World Series appearance since the "fixed" Series of 1919. Three trips to the playoffs after 1959 also resulted in failure. Former Sox shortstop Ozzie Guillen's hiring as manger in 2004 did not immediately work out.

Catcher A. J. Pierzynski jumps into closer Bobby Jenks's arms as third baseman Joe Crede joins the celebration on October 26, 2005. The White Sox had just defeated the Astros 1–0 to earn a World Series sweep.

OZZIE GUILLEN

On May 4, 2010, Ozzie Guillen managed his 1,000th game for the White Sox. It did not turn out as he had hoped—a 7–2 loss to the Kansas City Royals at U.S. Cellular Field. But Guillen was proud that he had lasted seven seasons as manager. That was longer than any other White Sox manager since Tony La Russa, who led the team from 1979 to 1986.

"I'm just lucky," the outspoken Guillen said. "The front office and [team chairman Jerry Reinsdorf] gave me good ballclubs. That's the only way you can stay. Most of the time managers get fired. They gave me the opportunity."

Guillen, a native of Venezuela, was a big-league shortstop from 1985 to 2000. He played his first 13 seasons with the White Sox. After his playing career, he was a coach with the Montreal Expos and the Florida Marlins until the White Sox hired him before the 2004 season.

But the White Sox won it all in Guillen's second season in charge. This was thanks to many factors. General manager Kenny Williams, for example, shook up the roster. He subtracted some of the team's power for speed. He traded slugging left fielder Carlos Lee to the Milwaukee Brewers for outfielder Scott Podsednik. Podsednik would become the team's speedy leadoff man. Another Sox fixture, right fielder Magglio Ordonez, left as a free agent for the Detroit Tigers. The Sox signed right fielder Jermaine Dye to take Ordonez's place. Podsednik and Dye would play key roles in the regular season and in the postseason.

Other new faces became contributors to the team's success. The Sox started the 2005 season with Shingo Takatsu of Japan as their closer.

Scott Podsednik, who was in his first season with the White Sox in 2005, helped Chicago with his speed. He stole 59 bases that season.

But Dustin Hermanson soon replaced him. When Hermanson developed back problems, the Sox turned to rookie Bobby Jenks. Jenks had a troubled career in the Los Angeles Angels' minor league system. But he was outstanding as a closer for the White Sox.

The Sox also employed another Japanese player—second baseman Tadahito Iguchi. He had been a power hitter in Japan before he signed with Chicago prior to the 2005 season. But Guillen needed a hitter to bat second. Iguchi adjusted his style and hit behind Podsednik.

In the starting rotation, former New York Yankee Jose Contreras blossomed under pitching coach Don Cooper's direction. Contreras and fellow Cuba native Orlando "El Duque" Hernandez, also an ex-Yankee, gave the rotation depth. Longtime starters Mark Buehrle and Jon Garland continued to excel. Freddy Garcia, a former Seattle Mariner whom the White Sox acquired in 2004, rounded out the starting five.

The Sox started out 2005 as if they would breeze to the American League (AL) Central title. They held a 15-game lead on August 1. But then the Cleveland Indians got hot. By September 22, the Sox's lead was down to 1 1/2 games. Chicago, however, pulled away to finish 99–63 and capture the division title by six games.

"If you said before the season that we were going to win the division, you're lying," Sox first baseman Paul Konerko said.

But the Sox believed in themselves and adopted the song "Don't Stop Believin'" by 1980s rock band Journey as their unofficial anthem. The song would ring in every Sox fan's ears throughout October 2005.

The White Sox faced the Boston Red Sox in the AL Division Series (ALDS). Chicago returned to midseason form. In the first two games, the White Sox beat the Red Sox 14–2 and 5–4 at U.S. Cellular Field. Chicago then won 5–3 in Game 3 at Fenway Park to sweep the series in three games.

In the AL Championship Series (ALCS) against the Los Angeles Angels, exceptional pitching boosted the White Sox. Chicago dropped Game 1 at home 3–2. But then the Sox's

Jose Contreras pitches in Game 5 of the 2005 ALCS. Contreras hurled the
White Sox's fourth straight complete game as they beat the Angels 6–3
and clinched a World Series berth.

rotation spun off four straight complete-game wins. Buehrle, Garland, Garcia, and Contreras recorded them. Contreras allowed just five hits in Game 5 as Chicago won 6–3 on the road to clinch a World Series berth.

The first World Series in the city of Chicago since 1959 opened at U.S. Cellular Field on October 22. The Sox's opponents were the Houston Astros. The Astros were appearing in their first World Series.

Dye got the Sox off to a great start in the first inning of Game 1. He hit an opposite-field solo homer off Astros ace

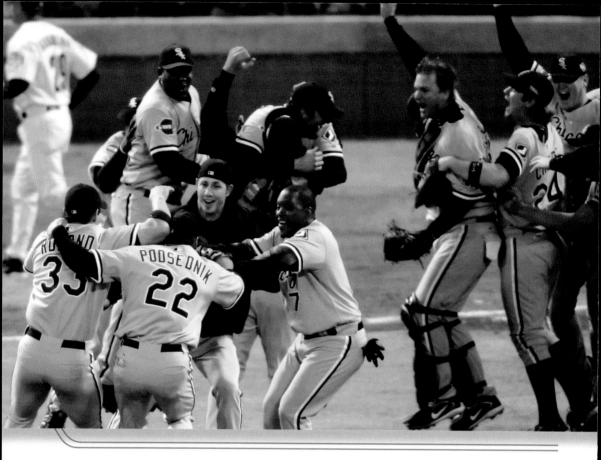

The White Sox celebrate after winning the 2005 World Series. It was the Sox's first Series title since 1917.

Roger Clemens. Chicago held on to win 5–3. In Game 2, Konerko hit the 18th grand slam in World Series history to rally the Sox from a 4–2 deficit in the seventh. The Astros tied the score at 6–6 in the ninth. But in the bottom half of the inning, Podsednik belted a pitch from Astros closer Brad Lidge to right-center. The result was a game-winning solo homer.

"Walking up to the plate, I was thinking more along the lines of slapping a base hit to left and stealing second," Podsednik said.

The Series moved to Minute Maid Park in Houston for Game 3. The Sox had to work overtime to earn a victory. They scored five runs in the fourth inning. But that is all they could muster as the game remained tied at 5–5 going into extra innings. Finally, in the top of the 14th, Geoff Blum hit a go-ahead solo homer into the right-field seats. Chicago ended up winning 7–5. "It's the stuff dreams are made of," said Blum, who entered the game in the 13th inning as a substitute.

The Sox then completed a remarkable postseason run with a four-game sweep of the Astros, winning 1–0 in Game 4. Garcia and three relievers limited Houston to five hits. The Sox were world champions. It was the team's third title overall.

Chicago finished 11–1 in the postseason. Dye earned World Series Most Valuable Player (MVP) honors. He finished the Series 7-for-16 for a .438 batting average with one homer and three runs batted in (RBIs).

The White Sox returned home. Two days after their title-clinching win, they were treated to a victory parade through downtown Chicago and nearby neighborhoods. An estimated 2 million people turned out.

The fans cherished the memories. Nobody could ever say again that a Chicago baseball team could not win it all.

CHAPTER 2

COMISKEY AND COMPANY

Chicago native Charles Comiskey was a groundbreaking first baseman. In his playing days in the 1880s with the St. Louis Browns of the American Association, he pioneered the defensive stance of playing off the bag to cut off grounders to the right side.

Comiskey moved over to the management side with the St. Paul Saints of the Western League in the late 1890s. Comiskey soon believed his ballclub should be elevated to major league status.

In partnership with Ban Johnson, president of the Western League, Comiskey sought in 1899 to found a new major league to compete with the established National League (NL). First, an agreement was made to shift the Saints to Chicago. Comiskey had to agree with James Hart, owner of the established Chicago Orphans, to play his home games south of 35th Street. The Orphans

Charles Comiskey owned the White Sox from the team's first season in 1900 until his death in 1931 and helped found the AL.

would later be renamed the Cubs. Comiskey's team played on a converted cricket field at 39th Street and Wentworth Avenue.

The realigned Western League was renamed the AL in 1900. In 1901, Johnson, Comiskey, and other executives regarded the new AL as

The Sox's Early Ace

"Big Ed" Walsh, the White Sox's greatest ace of the first two decades of the twentieth century, had four seasons in which he recorded at least 24 victories. Topping them all was his 40–15 year in 1908. Walsh's "out" pitch was the spitball, delivered with a variety of substances applied to the ball to make it dip and dart. The spitball was legal at the time. Walsh also hurled the first no-hitter at Comiskey Park, a 5–0 victory over the Boston Red Sox on August 27, 1911. Walsh played in the big leagues from 1904 to 1917. All but his final season were played with the White Sox. He finished with a career record of 195–126.

another major league. Comiskey renamed his club the White Stockings. The nickname had been abandoned by the Orphans years earlier.

Comiskey hired Clark Griffith to succeed him as manager in 1901. Pitching became the White Stockings' strength. The team's nickname was shortened to White Sox in 1904.

The 1906 Sox were not even considered the most talented of the franchise's teams. They batted only .230 with just seven homers as a team. But they won games thanks to ace pitchers such as Frank Owen, Nick Altrock, "Big Ed" Walsh, and Doc White. The pitchers tossed 32 shutouts. The Sox themselves were blanked 16 times. Manager Fielder Jones's team acquired the nickname "Hitless Wonders."

After winning the AL pennant, the Sox faced the

"Big Ed" Walsh, shown in 1908, was a star pitcher for the White Sox from 1904 to 1916. He helped the team capture the 1906 World Series title.

powerful Cubs in the World Series. Through 2010, the 1906 matchup was still the only Fall Classic duel between the cross-town rivals. The Cubs had won a record 116 regular-season games. The Sox benefited from Walsh's two-hit shutout to win 3–0 in Game 3. Then the team's offense unexpectedly erupted in Games 5 and 6. The Sox won 8–6 and 8–3 in those games to clinch the title.

The Sox could not repeat their startling success of 1906. But they did have some remarkable pitching achievements over the next decade. In 1908, Walsh started 49 games. He also appeared in relief in

Second baseman Eddie Collins joined the White Sox in 1915 and helped lead the team to a World Series title in 1917 over the New York Giants.

17 games. Walsh went an amazing 40–15.

Comiskey realized that the Sox had outgrown their 39th Street Grounds. He commissioned the building of a new concrete-and-steel stadium at the northeast corner of 35th Street and Shields Avenue. This was five miles south of downtown Chicago. Named after the owner, Comiskey Park opened amid grand ceremonies on July 1, 1910. The new ballpark's estimated cost was between $500,000 and $700,000.

The stadium was large for its time. An upper deck extended from first to third base.

The Sox stayed mediocre until 1915. Top second base-man Eddie Collins joined the team that year. Catcher Ray "Cracker" Schalk established himself behind the plate. Then the Sox made a huge acquisition on August 20, 1915. They paid $31,500 and sent three play-ers to the Cleveland Indians for outfielder "Shoeless" Joe Jack-son. He was considered one of the best hitters in the game after batting .408 in 1911. The move would pay off for Chicago. Jackson batted at least .341 in three full seasons with the Sox.

Comiskey's acquisitions helped turn Chicago into a top team. In 1917, managed by Clarence "Pants" Rowland, the Sox finished nine games in front of the AL pack with a 100–54 record. Right-hander

Eddie Cicotte was 28–12 with a 1.53 earned-run average (ERA). Chicago was more than prepared to duel manager John McGraw's powerful New York Giants in the World Series.

Honoring the US entry into World War I, the Sox opened the World Series with special ceremonies at Comis-key Park. Chicago won 2–1 in Game 1 behind Cicotte and 7–2 in Game 2 behind Urban "Red" Faber. The Giants then tied the Fall Classic as the Sox were shut out in Games 3 and 4 in New York. But the Sox came back and battered Giants pitch-ing for 14 hits in Game 5 in Chicago, winning 8–5. The Sox polished off the Giants back in New York, prevailing 4–2 on Faber's six-hitter.

Some very strange events would make the 1917 title their last world championship for 88 years.

CHAPTER 3

"BLACK SOX" AND A DARK ERA

The 1919 White Sox were baseball's strongest team that year. They probably were the best team in White Sox history.

Outfielder Joe Jackson batted .351 with 96 RBIs, 31 doubles, and 14 triples. Second baseman Eddie Collins hit .319 with 80 RBIs. The rest of the lineup was well balanced. The infield of Collins, first baseman Chick Gandil, shortstop "Swede" Risberg, and third baseman Buck Weaver was great defensively. Ace Eddie Cicotte went 29–7 with a 1.82 ERA. Claude "Lefty" Williams finished 23–11. The Sox easily won the AL pennant.

"There isn't any weak spot on my infield," rookie Sox manager William "Kid" Gleason

"Shoeless" Joe Jackson was a White Sox star from 1915 to 1920. However, the outfielder was banned from baseball as a result of the "Black Sox Scandal" that tarnished the 1919 World Series.

White Sox ace Eddie Cicotte took part in "fixing" the 1919 World Series. Cicotte was the losing pitcher in two games as the Cincinnati Reds won the Series five games to three.

said. "Take those four fellows with Ray Schalk behind the plate, and I don't know how they can be beaten."

However, behind the scenes, several players did display a weak spot. Gambling on baseball, including by the players themselves, had been present since the beginnings of the game. As the season drew to a close on September 18, 1919, Gandil contacted gambler Joseph "Sport" Sullivan in a Boston hotel. They discussed the idea of "fixing" the upcoming World Series. Sullivan acted as a representative for New York's Arnold Rothstein, the country's top gambler. The idea was to give the White Sox $100,000 to "throw," or lose on purpose, the World Series to the Cincinnati Reds. Gandil then met with several of his teammates about the plan. Many of the players thought owner Charles Comiskey underpaid them and thus they needed to engage in this illegal activity. The truth was Comiskey paid the going rate for player salaries in 1919.

The gamblers gave just $10,000 to the players as the World Series, expanded to nine games for that season, got underway. All the money went to Cicotte. He signaled that the "fix" was on by hitting the first Reds batter of the game in Cincinnati. The game featured bad pitching by Cicotte and only six hits by the White Sox. The Sox lost 9–1. They also lost 4–2 in Game 2. Chicago then played its usual

JACKSON'S GRAND FINALE

"Shoeless" Joe Jackson's final season in 1920 was sensational. He compiled 218 hits, good for a .382 batting average. Jackson had 42 doubles, 20 triples, and 12 homers. He drove in 121 runs and scored 105.

In six White Sox seasons, Jackson hit .356. For his career, Jackson batted .356 over parts of 13 seasons with three teams. Through 2010, Jackson's .356 career average was the third highest in baseball history. Only Ty Cobb (.366) and Rogers Hornsby (.358) had better averages.

Despite his many accomplishments, Jackson was never allowed into the Baseball Hall of Fame because of his ban from the sport following his involvement in the "Black Sox Scandal."

game in a 3–0 win in Game 3. Cicotte made two misplays in a two-run Reds fifth inning in Game 4 as the series shifted to Comiskey Park. Chicago lost 2–0. The Sox then fell 5–0 in Game 5. Stunned fans and sportswriters wondered why the Sox played so poorly.

By then, the Sox players were angered because the gamblers failed to pay them the money as agreed. They played legitimately in Game 6. They

rallied from a 4–0 deficit to win 5–4. Cicotte then finally pitched up to his standards. He scattered seven hits in a 4–1 win in Game 7. However, a gambler's "henchman" warned Williams, the Game 8 starter, that he and possibly his family would be harmed if he did not go along with the fix. Williams complied. He gave up four runs in just one-third of an inning as the Sox lost 10–5.

The scandal would become the worst in baseball history. Owner Charles Comiskey suspected something was wrong in Game 1. But his concern was dismissed by AL president Ban Johnson. Rumors of the fix continued throughout the following winter and into the 1920 season. The gamblers again pressured the Sox to throw games late in the 1920 season. This was after the team had taken a 3 1/2-game lead in

Home to Big Events

Comiskey Park was the site of several historic events in the 1930s. The first All-Star Game, timed to coincide with the World's Fair in Chicago, was held on July 6, 1933. Babe Ruth entertained the crowd with a home run. Joe Louis won the world heavyweight boxing championship against James J. Braddock on June 22, 1937. And on August 14, 1939, lights were turned on for night baseball at the ballpark as major league teams steadily added lights to transform the game.

Commissioner Kenesaw Mountain Landis, *rear left*, questions White Sox players during an investigation of the "Black Sox Scandal" in 1921. Landis suspended eight players from baseball for life.

the AL. Finally, a Cook County, Illinois, special grand jury was convened to investigate. Cicotte and Jackson finally admitted to Comiskey that they were in on the fix. With three games to go, the owner suspended the seven White Sox players—Cicotte, Jackson, Risberg, Williams, Weaver, outfielder "Happy"

Felsch, and infielder Freddie McMullin—who were still in the majors and thought to be involved in the scandal. Gandil had left the team after the 1919 season and was playing semi-pro ball.

"If you are guilty, you will be retired from organized baseball for the rest of your lives if

I can accomplish it," Comiskey told the banished players. A patchwork Sox lineup dropped two of the final three games while the Cleveland Indians won the pennant.

Kenesaw Mountain Landis was appointed commissioner by baseball owners eager to "clean up" the game. Landis suspended what were called the "Black Sox" players for life before the 1921 season. The eight players, including Gandil, had been acquitted in a conspiracy trial in Cook County. But they could no longer play any organized baseball. As a result, a sign is placed in every big-league clubhouse warning of lifetime suspensions for gambling on baseball.

Without his stars, Comiskey was forced to find players and piece together a team. The Sox dropped to 62–92 and seventh place in 1921. The Sox would not recover from the "Black Sox Scandal" for another three decades. Chicago would field just seven teams that had records above .500 until 1951.

The Sox still had great players, though. Shortstop Luke Appling made his debut in 1930. He went on to play 20 seasons with a lifetime average of .310 and a team-record 2,749 hits. Appling won AL batting titles in 1936 and 1943. He was elected to the Baseball Hall of Fame in 1964. Meanwhile, right-hander Ted Lyons came up in 1923. He went on to win 259 games through 1942. Lyons came back briefly after World War II to chalk up one more win in 1946. He had three 20-win seasons for mediocre teams. He preceded Appling into the Hall of Fame in 1955.

Team ownership moved through several generations of Comiskeys. Charles Comiskey

Hall of Fame shortstop Luke Appling, shown in 1940, spent his entire career, from 1930 to 1943 and then 1945 to 1950, with the White Sox. The team never finished better than third place during that time.

died on October 26, 1931. His son, J. Louis Comiskey, took over. But he lasted just eight years at the helm of the team because of frequent illness. J. Louis Comiskey died on July 18, 1939, at the age of 55. His widow, Grace Reidy Comiskey, took over the team in 1940. Eventually, her son Charley ran the club on a day-to-day basis. Frank Lane was hired as general manager for the 1949 season. He would be nicknamed "Trader Lane" for making many deals. Some of the trades brought the players who would revive the White Sox for the 1950s.

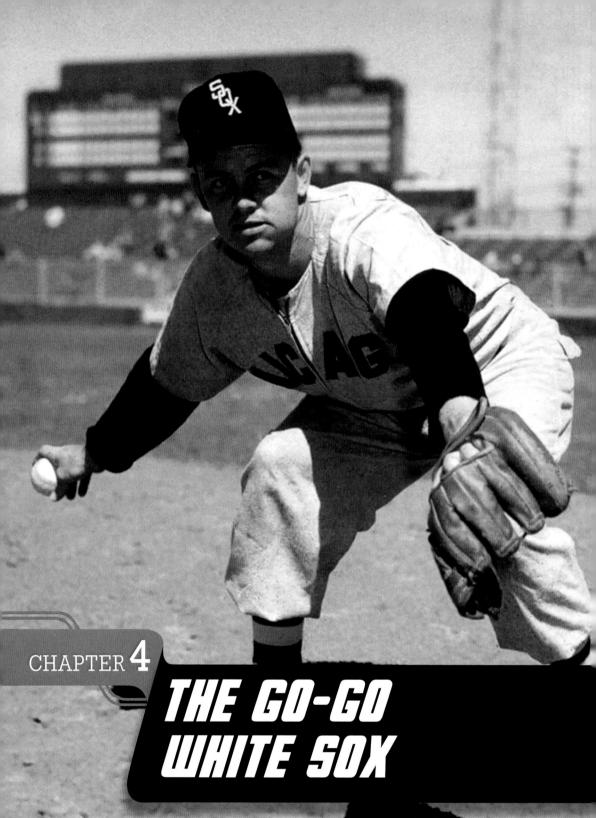

CHAPTER 4

THE GO-GO WHITE SOX

It did not immediately show up in the team's record. But the management team of Charley Comiskey and general manager Frank Lane was improving the White Sox as the 1950s began.

For the 1950 season, Lane acquired little second baseman Nellie Fox from the Philadelphia Athletics. The 5-foot-9 Fox would turn out to be the heart and soul of the Sox for the next 14 seasons. Also newly arriving were first baseman Eddie Robinson from the Washington Senators and shortstop Chico Carrasquel from the Brooklyn Dodgers' farm system. At season's end, Chicago hired Paul Richards as its skipper.

Richards revived the White Sox in 1951. Speedy Jim Busby took over in center field. Then Lane made a great trade on

Second baseman Nellie Fox, shown in 1953, was a White Sox star from 1950 to 1963. The team finished above .500 in the final 13 of those years.

April 30, 1951. He acquired outfielder Minnie Minoso from the Cleveland Indians. The Cuba native became the first black player for the Sox. Minoso batted .324 with 74 RBIs and 31 stolen bases for the season. Fox hit .313. Fans started chanting "go . . . go . . . go" whenever Minoso or Busby (26 steals) would get on base. The team became known as the "Go-Go Sox."

The Sox stunned the baseball world by winning 14 games in a row in May 1951. They did not have the staying power to keep up with the New York Yankees, however, and ended up in fourth place. But they established themselves as a competitive team. Under Richards, Chicago finished in third place each year from 1952 to 1954.

Richards left to take over the Baltimore Orioles as both general manager and field manager. Under new manager Marty Marion, the Sox finally challenged the Yankees for first place going into September 1955. They also challenged the Yankees in 1956 and 1957. But again Chicago fell short. By then, the Sox had yet another new manager. He was Al Lopez. Lopez led the Indians to the AL pennant in 1954. Chicago also had a new shortstop in speedy Luis Aparicio. He was a defensively gifted player who won the AL Rookie of the Year Award in 1956. Left-hander Billy Pierce, who had pitched for the Sox since 1949, won 20 games in both 1956 and 1957.

Changes off and on the field took place in 1959. Famed baseball showman Bill Veeck and partners bought majority control of the Sox on March 10, 1959. On the field, the Sox did not seem to be in great shape to

Left to right, White Sox shortstop Chico Carrasquel, outfielder Minnie Minoso, and pitcher Luis Aloma pose in 1951. Chicago finished 81–73 that year for its first winning season since 1943.

challenge the mighty Yankees again. They had few big run producers. But they caught a break. The Yankees were hampered by injuries and contract holdouts.

The 1959 Sox used the formula of pitching, speed, and defense. Aparicio stole an AL-leading 56 bases as the leadoff hitter. Fox batted second. He hit .306 and reached 70 RBIs

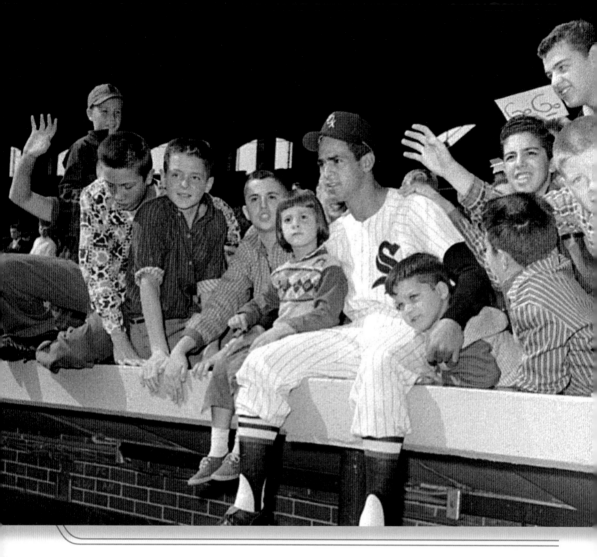

Shortstop Luis Aparicio sits atop a dugout at Comiskey Park on September 29, 1959. He is surrounded by young fans who were admitted free to attend a White Sox workout in preparation for the World Series.

despite hitting just two homers. He received the AL MVP Award. Early Wynn, who was a big winner for Lopez in Cleveland, finished 22–10.

The Sox went 94–60 and won the team's first pennant in 40 years. The bad memories of the "Black Sox" would be forgotten for now.

The Sox seemed to be the favorites to beat the Los Angeles Dodgers in the World Series. And they rolled to an 11–0 victory in Game 1 on October 1 at Comiskey Park. First baseman Ted Klusze-wski belted two homers. Kluszewski was known for cutting off the sleeves on his uniform, showing off his huge biceps. Wynn pitched shutout ball over seven innings. But the Sox were not as lucky in Game 2. They lost 4–3. On a key play, slow-footed Sher-man Lollar was easily thrown out at the plate on Al Smith's double with nobody out in the eighth.

The Dodgers' relief pitch-ing enabled them to win 3–1 and 5–4 in Games 3 and 4 in Los Angeles. But right-hander Bob Shaw outdueled a young Sandy Koufax 1–0 in Game 5 to send the World Series back

GREAT PROMOTER

White Sox owner Bill Veeck introduced the first exploding score-board at Comiskey Park in 1960. The scoreboard shot off fireworks whenever a Sox player hit a homer. Many ballparks imitated the loud scoreboard, and it is now common.

Veeck, a Chicago native, gained a reputation for his promotions while he owned the Cleveland Indians and the St. Louis Browns in the 1940s and 1950s. He became head owner of the White Sox in 1959, then sold his share of the team in 1961. He returned as owner in 1975.

Veeck held maybe his most famous promotion in 1979 when he hosted "Disco Demolition Night" on July 12 at Comiskey Park. Fans were told to bring disco records to destroy between games of a doubleheader. When the crowd got out of hand, the White Sox had to forfeit the second game to the Detroit Tigers. Veeck sold the Sox in 1981 and retired.

to Comiskey Park. That proved only a delay in the inevitable. The Sox were thrashed 9–3 in Game 6 on October 8.

Before the 1960 season, Veeck traded several key young players for older veterans. But the strategy did not work. In 1961, Veeck, who was ill, sold the team to Arthur C. Allyn.

Staying in Chicago

The Sox were under consideration to move out of Chicago at least three times between 1968 and 1980. Future commissioner Bud Selig tried to bring a team to Milwaukee to replace the Braves. He invited the Sox to play a number of games at County Stadium in 1968 and 1969. Instead of the Sox, Selig bought the bankrupt Seattle Pilots and moved them to Milwaukee in 1970. Later, in 1975, the Sox were thought to be Seattle-bound as a replacement team for the Pilots. But Bill Veeck bought the team before a move could be seriously considered. When Veeck sought to sell the Sox in 1980, he talked with Denver oilman Marvin Davis. But those talks did not result in a deal.

The Sox rebounded and won at least 94 games each season from 1963 to 1965. In 1967, the Sox missed a golden chance to win the pennant. Chicago was among four AL teams vying for the flag. But the Sox lost their final five games.

The 1967 flop sent the Sox into a nosedive. Chicago fell all the way to 56–106 in 1970. The club then began a revival that shifted into high gear when the team acquired slugger Dick Allen from the Dodgers. Allen won the AL MVP Award in 1972 with 37 homers and 113 RBIs.

In 1972, the Sox battled the eventual world champion Oakland Athletics for the AL West title into September before falling out of contention. Allen then broke his leg during the 1973 season. He quit the team near the end of the 1974 campaign. The Sox declined again and nearly went bankrupt. But

White Sox slugger Ted Kluszewski watches one of his two home runs in Game 1 of the 1959 World Series. Chicago beat the Los Angeles Dodgers 11–0 in that game but lost the Series in six games.

Veeck saved them a second time. He rounded up a group of investors late in 1975 to buy the team.

Veeck used a "rent-a-player" strategy to forge a memorable summer of 1977. The "South Side Hit Men" held first place into August. But the team faded to a third-place finish. Oscar Gamble had 31 homers and Richie Zisk added 30. But both players departed as free agents before the next season.

The fortunes of the Sox went down again. Veeck looked to sell. But before he departed as owner for the last time, he hired a future great manager. The Sox's roller coaster would continue under Tony La Russa as the 1980s began.

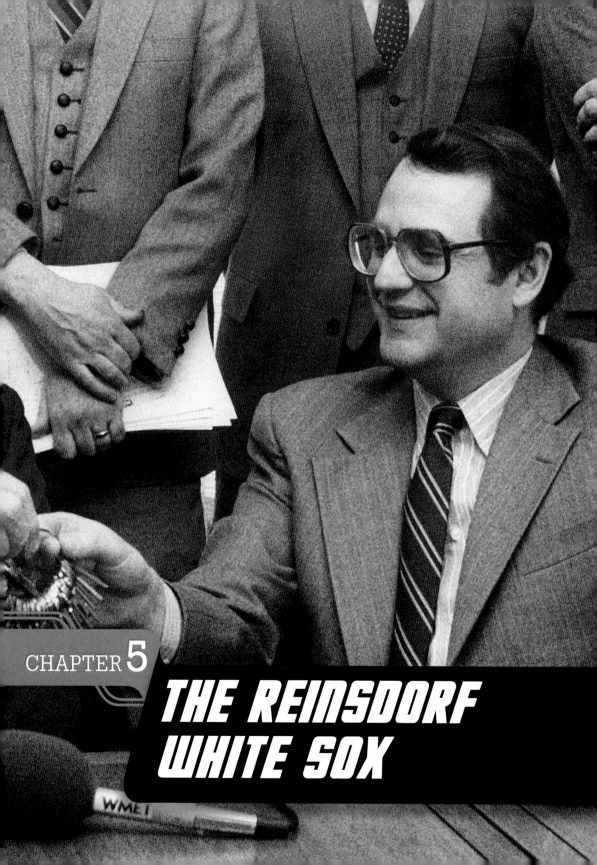

CHAPTER 5

THE REINSDORF WHITE SOX

By the late 1970s, White Sox owner Bill Veeck was looking to save money. As a result, on August 2, 1979, he hired Tony La Russa, his Triple-A manager, to run the Sox. La Russa, just 34 years old, replaced Don Kessinger.

Some critics wondered why such a young, inexperienced man was given the job. But they soon found out that La Russa, a former big-league infielder, was smart and tough.

Before the 1981 season, Veeck sold the team to an ownership group headed by real estate executive Jerry Reinsdorf of Chicago and TV sports businessman Eddie Einhorn of New Jersey.

Reinsdorf and Einhorn made immediate improvements. The Sox picked up sluggers Carlton Fisk, a former Boston Red Sox star, and Greg Luzinski, formerly of the Philadelphia Phillies.

New White Sox owner Jerry Reinsdorf receives the keys to Comiskey Park in 1981. As of 2010, Reinsdorf still owned the team.

The Sox were competitive again. They had winning records in the strike-shortened season of 1981 and in 1982. In 1983, they won the AL West by a record 20 games. Chicago finished 99–63. Hometown slugger Ron Kittle complemented Fisk and Luzinski. Kittle's 35 homers and 100 RBIs won him the AL Rookie of the Year Award. Other standouts were outfielder Harold Baines, leadoff man Rudy Law, and pitchers LaMarr Hoyt, Richard Dotson, and Britt Burns. Law set a team record with 77 stolen bases. Hoyt went 24–10 and won the AL Cy Young Award.

The Sox got off to a promising start in the ALCS. They beat the Orioles 2–1 in Baltimore. But the Sox lost 4–0 in Game 2 as Orioles right-hander Mike Boddicker struck out 14. The series shifted to Comiskey Park. The Orioles cruised to an 11–1 victory in Game 3. Game 4 was scoreless into the 10th inning. Starter Burns remained in the game but served up a one-out homer to the Orioles' Tito Landrum. Baltimore scored two more runs in the 10th to win the game and the series.

The Sox went into a serious decline. They did, however, welcome a new shortstop in 1985. Venezuela native Ozzie Guillen took over the position and was voted AL Rookie of the Year. A year later, a promising outfielder joined the Sox. Ken Williams played three seasons on the South Side. He even performed alongside Guillen for a short time at third base in 1988. Guillen and Williams would be better known for other roles—as manager and general manager—with the White Sox almost two decades later.

La Russa was fired by general manager Ken "Hawk"

LaMarr Hoyt pitches in 1983. The AL Cy Young Award winner helped the White Sox reach the postseason for the first time since 1959.

Harrelson during the 1986 season. La Russa later was very successful managing the Oakland Athletics and the St. Louis Cardinals. Harrelson lasted just one year as general manager. Larry Himes succeeded him in 1987. While the Sox lost on the field, Himes struck gold on his number one draft choices. He selected pitcher Jack McDowell in 1987, third baseman Robin Ventura in 1988, first baseman Frank Thomas in 1989, and pitcher Alex Fernandez in 1990. Those players would soon form the core of a contending team.

But the biggest news of the late 1980s was the Sox's threat to move to St. Petersburg, Florida. Reinsdorf found that

Frank Thomas hits a run-scoring single during Game 3 of the 1993 ALCS against the Blue Jays. The White Sox lost the series in six games.

Comiskey Park was structurally poor and was a potential hazard to fans and players. A campaign began to get the Illinois state legislature to approve funding for a new stadium. Fans worried until the final deadline on July 1, 1988, that the Sox would leave town. But the legislature approved the stadium bill. Construction on the new Comiskey Park, across 35th Street from the old ballpark, began in 1989.

In the last year of the old ballpark, in 1990, the Sox staged a revival. They won 94 games to finish second in the AL West. The Sox contended in 1991 and 1992. They finally took off to win the AL West in 1993 under manager Gene Lamont. Thomas captured the league's MVP Award with

41 homers and 128 RBIs. McDowell went 22–10 and won the AL Cy Young Award. The Sox finished 94–68 and won the division. However, they lost in six games in the ALCS to the Toronto Blue Jays.

A players' strike in 1994 interrupted the Sox's momentum. The team was in first place when play was stopped on August 10. When the strike ended in 1995, the Sox could not resume their winning ways. Lamont was fired. The team was an also-ran for the rest of the 1990s despite great seasons from Thomas. Slugger Albert Belle was signed in 1997. The following year, he had 49 homers, 152 RBIs, and a .328 batting average.

Belle had departed as a free agent when the Sox surged to another AL West title in 2000. The team finished 95–67 under third-year

FRANK THOMAS

Frank Thomas had one of the best combinations of power and patience in baseball history.

Thomas had five seasons of 40 or more homers and 10 with 100 or more walks for the Sox between 1991 and 2003. Thomas led the AL in walks four times, with a high of 138 in 1991. He had eight consecutive seasons of 100 or more RBIs between 1991 and 1998. He was selected AL MVP in 1993 and 1994.

Thomas left the Sox in 2005 and finished his career with the Toronto Blue Jays and the Oakland Athletics. Thomas totaled 521 career homers with a .301 average. Even though he had a conflict with general manager Kenny Williams when he departed the Sox, the team honored him with a special day with the New York Yankees in town on August 29, 2010.

manager Jerry Manuel. A new group of young hitters, including outfielders Magglio Ordonez and Carlos Lee and first baseman Paul Konerko, were in the lineup by then. They complemented Thomas. However, the Seattle Mariners swept Chicago in three games in the ALDS.

More change took place after the 2000 season. Williams, the Sox's farm director, was promoted to general manager. Williams tinkered with the Sox for three more also-ran seasons. He then hired old teammate Guillen as manager and made several key trades that set up the 2005 season. And the rest was history as the team won its first World Series title in 88 years.

The White Sox went 90–72 in 2006 but could not repeat as division champions. They finished third in the AL Central. The White Sox had added pop by acquiring slugger Jim Thome from the Phillies before the season. He belted 42 home runs. But the Sox could not find the same magic that they had discovered in 2005.

In the five seasons after their amazing ride in 2005, the White Sox qualified for the postseason once. That was in 2008, when they won the AL Central by defeating the visiting Minnesota Twins 1–0 in a one-game tiebreaker. John Danks and Bobby Jenks combined on a shutout. However, the Sox lost three games to one

"Hawk" Harrelson's Nicknames

Sox television announcer Ken Harrelson, more popularly known as "Hawk," passed out nicknames to the players. Frank Thomas was called "The Big Hurt." Outfielder Lance Johnson became "One Dog." Pitcher Jack McDowell was "Black Jack." And outfielder Warren Newson was anointed "The Deacon."

White Sox manager Ozzie Guillen, *right*, and general manager Kenny Williams share a laugh in 2010. The two men helped lead the Sox to much success in the 2000s, including a World Series title in 2005.

to the Tampa Bay Rays in the ALDS.

Chicago contended for the AL Central crown in 2010. The Sox led the division in early August. But the Twins passed them down the stretch.

With Guillen and standout left-handed pitchers Danks and Mark Buehrle helping lead the way, the White Sox and their fans could be optimistic about the future. The team hoped that it could someday soon get back to the World Series and have a season as memorable as 2005.

TIMELINE

1900	The St. Paul Saints of the Western League move to Chicago and are renamed the White Stockings.
1901	The White Stockings play their first season in the new AL.
1906	Now called the White Sox, the team beats the visiting Chicago Cubs 8–3 on October 14 in Game 6 of the World Series to clinch the first title in franchise history.
1917	The Sox win their second World Series title in as many tries by defeating the New York Giants four games to two. Chicago beats host New York 4–2 on October 15 to clinch the crown.
1919	A group of Sox players fix the World Series against the Cincinnati Reds. Chicago loses the special best-of-nine Series five games to three. The Sox are forever branded "The Black Sox."
1931	Founding owner Charles Comiskey dies on October 26.
1959	The Sox win their first AL pennant since 1919, clinching it on September 22 with a 4–2 win over the host Cleveland Indians. Chicago, however, falls to the Los Angeles Dodgers in six games in the World Series.
1972	Dick Allen revives the Sox with his 37-homer, 113-RBI MVP season. Chicago finishes 87–67.
1981	Jerry Reinsdorf and Eddie Einhorn purchase the Sox from Bill Veeck.

1983	Chicago, led by AL Cy Young Award winner LaMarr Hoyt and AL Rookie of the Year Ron Kittle, finishes 99–63 under manager Tony La Russa and wins the AL West by a whopping 20 games. The White Sox, however, fall three games to one to the Baltimore Orioles in the ALCS.
1993	Chicago goes 94–68 and wins the AL West. League MVP Frank Thomas leads the way with 41 home runs. Jack McDowell captures the AL Cy Young Award. The Sox lose in six games to the Toronto Blue Jays in the ALCS.
2000	The Sox finish 95–67 and win the AL Central. Chicago, however, is swept in three games by the Seattle Mariners in the ALDS.
2003	On November 3, the White Sox hire Florida Marlins third-base coach Ozzie Guillen as their manager. Guillen played shortstop for the Sox from 1985 to 1997.
2005	Chicago goes 99–63 and captures the AL Central crown. The White Sox sweep the Boston Red Sox in three games in the ALDS, defeat the Los Angeles Angels four games to one in the ALCS, and then sweep the Houston Astros in four games to win the team's first World Series title since 1917.
2008	The Sox finish the regular schedule tied with the Minnesota Twins atop the AL Central at 88–74. John Danks combines with Bobby Jenks on a shutout as host Chicago defeats Minnesota 1–0 in a one-game tiebreaker to win the division title. The Sox fall three games to one to the Tampa Bay Rays in the ALDS.
2010	Chicago leads the AL Central in early August before Minnesota takes control of the race and wins by six games. The Sox finish second at 88–74.

QUICK STATS

FRANCHISE HISTORY
Chicago White Stockings (1901–03)
Chicago White Sox (1904–)

WORLD SERIES
(wins in bold)
1906, **1917**, 1919, 1959, **2005**

AL CHAMPIONSHIP SERIES
(1969–)
1983, 1993, 2005

DIVISION CHAMPIONSHIPS
(1969–)
1983, 1993, 2000, 2005, 2008

WILD-CARD BERTHS
(1995–)
None

KEY PLAYERS
(position[s]; seasons with team)
Luis Aparicio (SS; 1956–62, 1968–70)
Luke Appling (SS; 1930–43,
    1945–50)
Mark Buehrle (SP; 2000–)
Eddie Collins (2B; 1915–26)
Urban "Red" Faber (P; 1914–33)
Carlton Fisk (C; 1981–93)
Nellie Fox (2B; 1950–63)
Joe Jackson (OF; 1915–20)
Paul Konerko (1B; 1999–)
Ted Lyons (SP; 1923–42, 1946)
Minnie Minoso (OF; 1951–57,
    1961–62, 1964, 1976, 1980)
Billy Pierce (SP; 1949–61)
Frank Thomas (1B/DH; 1990–2005)
Ed Walsh (P; 1904–16)

KEY MANAGERS
Ozzie Guillen (2004–):
    600–535; 12–4 (postseason)
Al Lopez (1957–65, 1968–69):
    840–650; 2–4 (postseason)

HOME PARKS
39th Street Grounds (1901–10)
Comiskey Park I (1910–90)
U.S. Cellular Field (1991–)
    Known as Comiskey Park II
    (1991–2003)
* All statistics through 2010 season

QUOTES AND ANECDOTES

Through 2010, White Sox pitchers had thrown 17 no-hitters. But it is the two perfect games in team history that really stand out. Rookie Charlie Robertson went 27 up, 27 down against the Tigers on April 30, 1922, at Detroit. Eighty-five years later, the White Sox's Mark Buehrle astounded baseball fans by throwing a no-hitter against the Texas Rangers on April 18, 2007, at U.S. Cellular Field. But Buehrle provided an absolute shock on July 23, 2009, against the Tampa Bay Rays in Chicago. He took a perfect game into the ninth. Dewayne Wise, just inserted into center field, made a leaping catch above the fence to steal a potential leadoff homer in the ninth from Gabe Kapler. Relieved, Buehrle mowed down the final two hitters to nail the perfect game.

"The last two innings, my heart was pounding like crazy. I was so excited. So many people were waiting for this moment."
—Chicago manager Ozzie Guillen, after his team defeated the host Houston Astros 1–0 in Game 4 to sweep the 2005 World Series

Broadcaster Harry Caray started the famous seventh-inning singalong of "Take Me Out to the Ballgame" at the old Comiskey Park in 1977. Sox owner Bill Veeck spotted Caray singing to himself in the booth, so he persuaded Caray to let him share his off-key voice with the crowd. Caray's performance became an immediate hit. He moved it over to Wrigley Field when he became a broadcaster for the Cubs in 1982, and the singing act became bigger than ever.

Hall of Fame pitcher Tom Seaver joined the White Sox before the 1984 season. At the age of 39, he went 15–11 in 1984. The next year, the right-hander finished 16–11. He earned the 300th win of his career on August 4, 1985, when the Sox beat the host New York Yankees 4–1.

GLOSSARY

ace

A team's best starting pitcher.

acquire

To add a player, usually through the draft, free agency, or a trade.

berth

A place, spot, or position, such as in the baseball playoffs.

clinch

To officially settle something, such as a berth in the playoffs.

commissioner

A person authorized to perform certain tasks or endowed with certain powers.

farm system

A big-league club's teams in the minor leagues, where players are developed for the majors.

franchise

An entire sports organization, including the players, coaches, and staff.

general manager

The executive who is in charge of the team's overall operation. He or she hires and fires managers and coaches, drafts players, and signs free agents.

mediocre

Neither good nor bad.

pennant

A flag. In baseball, it symbolizes that a team has won its league championship.

retire

To officially end one's career.

rookie

A first-year player in the major leagues.

roster

The players as a whole on a baseball team.

veteran

An individual with great experience in a particular endeavor.

FOR MORE INFORMATION

Further Reading

Gonzales, Mark. *The Good, the Bad and the Ugly: Heart-Pounding, Jaw-Dropping, and Gut-Wrenching Moments from Chicago White Sox History*. Chicago: Triumph Books, 2009.

Kittle, Ron, with Bob Logan. *Tales from the White Sox Dugout*. Champaign, IL: Sports Publishing LLC, 2005.

Lindberg, Richard C. *Total White Sox*. Chicago: Triumph Books, 2006.

Web Links

To learn more about the Chicago White Sox, visit ABDO Publishing Company online at **www.abdopublishing.com**. Web sites about the White Sox are featured on our Book Links page. These links are routinely monitored and updated to provide the most current information available.

Places to Visit

National Baseball Hall of Fame and Museum
25 Main Street
Cooperstown, NY 13326
1-888-HALL-OF-FAME
www.baseballhall.org
This hall of fame and museum highlights the greatest players and moments in the history of baseball. Luis Aparicio, Eddie Collins, Carlton Fisk, Nellie Fox, and Ed Walsh are among the former White Sox players enshrined here.

U.S. Cellular Field
333 W. 35th Street
Chicago, IL 60613
312-674-1000
http://mlb.mlb.com/cws/ballpark/index.jsp
This has been the White Sox's home field since 1991. The team plays 81 regular-season games here each year.

White Sox Spring Training
Camelback Ranch
10710 W. Camelback Road
Glendale, AZ 85037
623-302-5200
http://camelbackranchbaseball.com
This has been the White Sox's spring-training ballpark since 2009.

INDEX

About the Author

George Castle is a lifelong Chicagoan. Castle has covered Chicago baseball for a variety of media outlets since 1980. He has authored 11 baseball books since 1998, hosts the syndicated weekly Diamond Gems radio show, and writes for numerous print and online outlets.